The Elep Child

Written by
Jill Atkins

Illustrated by
Gordy Wright

Long, long ago, elephants did not have long trunks.

They all had big black snouts, which were not very useful.

One day, a new elephant was born. He was called the elephant's child!

He wanted to find out everything.

"Why do your tail feathers grow like that?" he asked the ostrich.

The ostrich pecked at him with her sharp beak.

"Go away!" she snapped.

"Why is your hump so big?" he asked the camel.

The camel bent over him and frowned.

"Go away!" he growled.

"Why are your eyes so red?" he asked the hippo.

The hippo opened her mouth wide.

"Go away," she snarled.

Then one day, his mum told him about crocodiles.

"What do crocodiles have for dinner?" he asked.

"Sh!" cried his mum. "You must not speak of that!"

But a Kolokolo bird hopped up to the elephant's child.

"Go to the big, wide river," she screeched. "There you will find out."

She knew the elephant's child would go to the river.

Off went the elephant's child. He walked until he came to the big, wide river.

There he met a snake.

"Have you seen a crocodile?" asked the elephant's child.

"Yes," said the snake. "I have seen a few. The crocodile means danger."

The elephant's child had never seen a crocodile. So when he stepped on a log, he was surprised when the log winked at him.

Then it blinked and flicked its tail.

"Excuse me, but will you tell me what crocodiles have for dinner?" asked the elephant's child.

"I am the crocodile," snapped the log, with a toothy grin. "I will show you what I have for dinner."

Then he grabbed the elephant's child's nose.

"Ow!" cried the elephant's child.

The crocodile tugged hard, so the snake rushed to help the elephant's child.

As they tugged, the elephant's child's nose began to grow. It grew longer and longer.

After a long while, the crocodile let go and the elephant's child fell back onto the river bank.

"Thank you, Snake. You rescued me," said the elephant's child, as the snake slithered away.

All day, the elephant's child waited for his long trunk to shrink!

But while he waited, he found that this new trunk was very useful!

When he arrived back at the herd, all the elephants admired his trunk.

So they all set off to the big, wide river to visit the crocodile.

And from that day on, all elephants had long, useful trunks!